BUILDINGS

Betsey Chessen
Pamela Chanko

Scholastic Ltd

Design: Silver Editions

Photo Research: Silver Editions

Endnotes: Susan Russell

Endnote Illustrations: Hokanson/Cichetti

Photographs: Cover: David Hiser/Tony Stone Images; p. 1: (tl) David Hiser/Tony Stone Images; (tr) Joe Sohm/Photo Researchers, Inc.; (bl) Jeff Greenberg/Photo Researchers, Inc.; (br) Chris Thomaidis/Tony Stone Images; p. 2: Joe Sohm/Photo Researchers, Inc.; p. 3: Tony Stone Images; p. 4: Noboru Komine/Photo Researchers, Inc.; p. 5: Jeff Greenberg/Photo Researchers, Inc.; p. 6: John Moss/Photo Researchers, Inc.; p. 7: Sylvain Grandadam/Tony Stone Images; p. 8: Chris Thomaidis/Tony Stone Images; p. 9: David Hiser/Tony Stone Images; p. 10: Kenneth Murray/Photo Researchers, Inc.; p. 11: David Robbins/Tony Stone Images; p. 12: Hilarie Kavanagh/Tony Stone Images.

© 1998 by Scholastic Inc.

This edition © 2001 by Scholastic Ltd, Villiers House, Clarendon Avenue, Leamington Spa, Warwickshire CV32 5PR

British Library Cataloguing-in-Publication Data. A catalogue record for this book is available from the British Library.

ISBN 0-439-01944-3

Printed by Lynx Offset Ltd, Chalgrove.

1 2 3 4 5 6 7 8 9 0   1 2 3 4 5 6 7 8 9 0

What are buildings made of?

Some are made of wood.

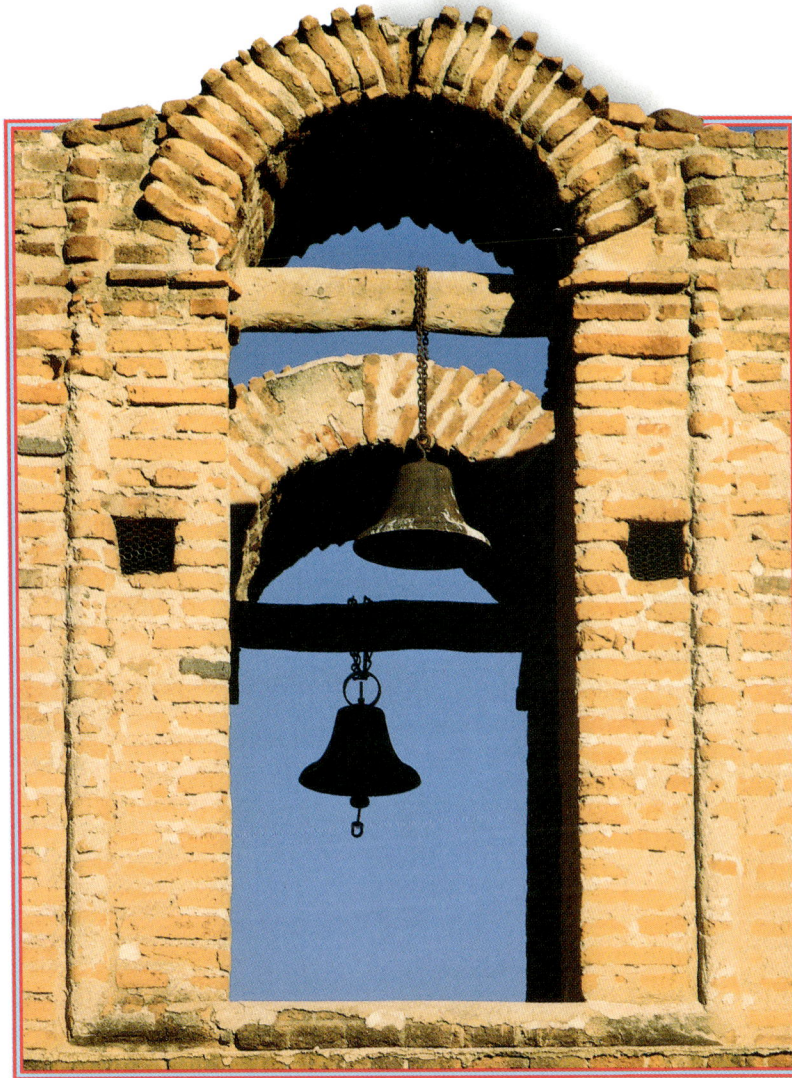

Some are made of brick.

Some are made of rock.

Some are made of stone.

Some are made of metal.

Some are made of mud.

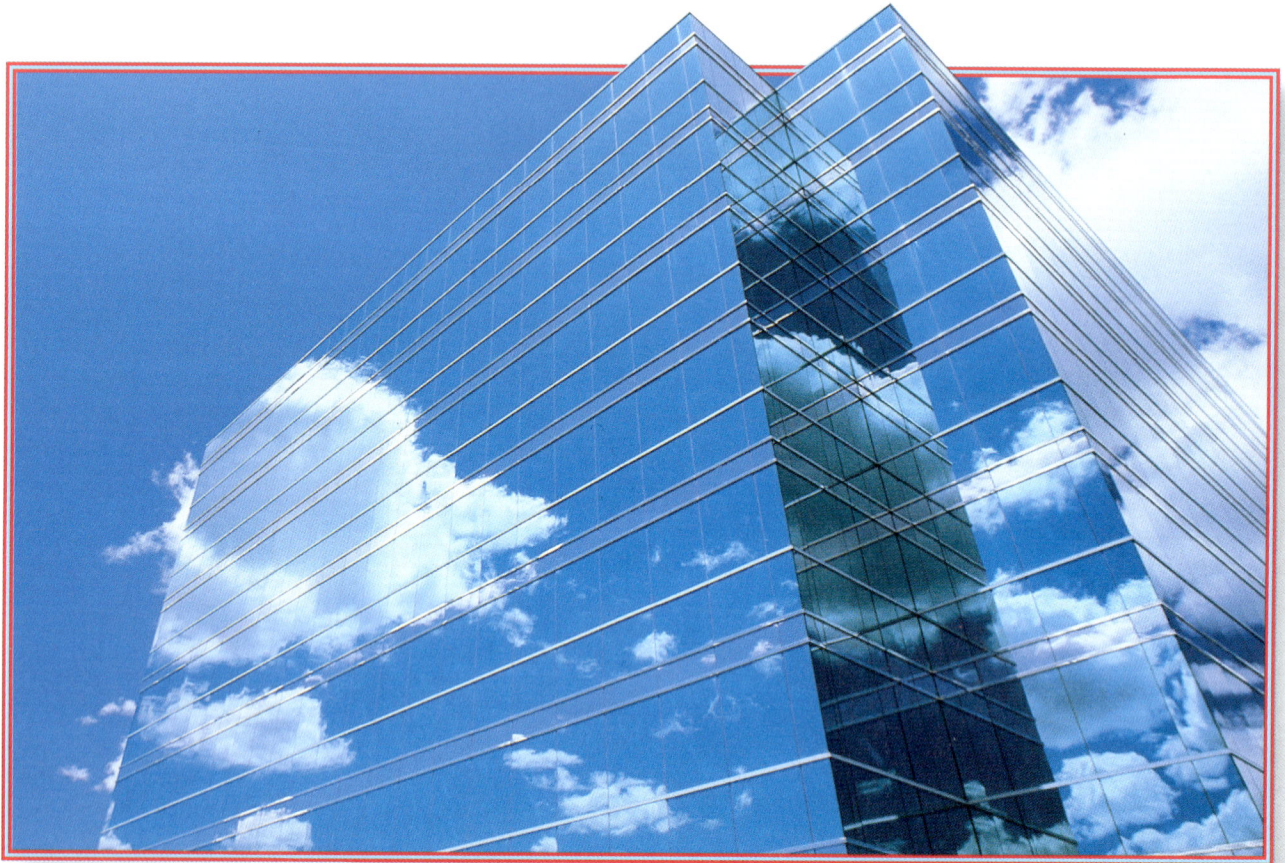

Some are made of glass.

Some are made of ice.

Some are made of straw.

Some are made of logs.

Some are even made of gold.

BUILDINGS

Buildings can be made from many different materials. Wood, bricks and stone are just a few. Sometimes a building is made of several different materials in combination. The material a building is made of often depends on what the building will be used for and in what environment it is built. Will it be a place to work or a place to live? Is it in the desert or in a big city? The answers to these questions help the builders decide what materials to use.

Wood   Wood has always been a basic building material for people who live in temperate climates, where lots of trees grow. This building is a barn in Vermont in the USA. It is used as a shelter for animals like cows and horses.

Brick   People first made bricks by baking dirt and clay. They were fairly small so that they could be easily thrown up to the mason who was working high up on the wall. This building is a bell tower in New Mexico.

Rock   Long ago, some people built shelters right into the sides of huge rocks. These small rooms kept people protected from the weather. Some of them are still inhabited today. These buildings are in a village in Turkey called Uchisar. The quarters are actually used for restaurants and tourist accommodation!

Stone   Sometimes builders take small stones and use them like bricks, joining them together with mortar to form walls. The strength of such buildings lies in their weight. All those stones are very heavy! This stone house is in Alabama in the USA.

Metal When people discovered how to make cast iron, architects began designing very different buildings. Metal is both lighter and stronger than stone, and can support great weight. Therefore, buildings made of metal can be very tall. This is the famous Eiffel Tower in Paris.

Mud This mud house is very practical in its environment, which is the desert. Dried mud makes a long-lasting house here because it doesn't rain. This house is in the Moroccan desert.

Glass In the mid-twentieth century people began to erect buildings that had metal skeletons and were covered on the outside with glass. They always use a special kind of glass, very thick and strong. If you look up in a big city, you can see skyscrapers like this one reflecting the clouds.

Ice People who live in very cold, frozen climates also use what is close by to create buildings. They cut blocks of ice from the frozen ground to make bricks they can stack. These homes are called igloos. This one is in the Northwest Territories in Canada.

Straw One of the building materials used in this small church in Peru is straw. The building is in an area too high for trees to grow, where straw was easier to find than wood. The thin reeds were laid side by side and sewn together to form a lightweight roof and walls. This straw building is on an island in Lake Titicaca, the highest lake in the world.

Logs Pioneers who didn't have a way to saw the tree trunks into boards used the whole log as a building material instead. These logs were fitted together to build strong walls and roofs. This log cabin is in the woods of Alaska in the USA.

Gold Very few buildings in the world use gold as a building material. This amazing structure is the Shwe Dagon Palace in Rangoon, Burma. Its tall, cone-shaped towers are completely covered in gold!